# Shifting Paradigms For Men Transformation Through Renewed Vision Student Workbook

by

LuVara R. Prudhomme

Copyright © 2016, LuVara R. Prudhomme www.yourmindshift.com

All rights reserved. No part of this book may be reproduced, stored, or transmitted by any means— whether auditory, graphic, mechanical, or electronic—without written permission of both publisher and author, except in the case of brief excerpts used in critical articles and reviews. Unauthorized reproduction of any part of this work is illegal and is punishable by law.

ISBN 978-0-9908859-6-2

# FOREWORD

Shifting Paradigms Series is the good news that answers so many dark questions of life that so often overshadow ones dreams and bankrupts their faith account. This guide is a balance of personal experience, backed by a biblical foundation that seals the power to apply.

Each of us who take on the challenge to use this instructive guiding light of hope to illuminate misguided pathways and increase self-awareness are empowered to shift the platform of our outlook on life. This shining moment could not have presented itself at a greater time than now.

LuVara's universal, personal and Christ-centered experiences afford her the ability to unleash a dramatic outlook on the core of life and the human process that leads to personal inventory. Readers are given a chance to fill in the blank spaces within their own lives. This is what I call "turn the corner of life", where the reader is brought to the well to drink of the author's rich experience but leave with a taste of their own as their pail of reality is drawn from the well of life.

We are thankful for her tenacity to release the God given gift so that others may be blessed as she pushes the margin and raises the bar on life's greater expectations. By allowing God to push and guide her pen to produce the life rays of hope that beams into the lives of others, her work unearths the treasure deep within.

It has been my privilege to interact with LuVara through her efforts to address the issues as is. Through the art of keeping it real, the facts and feelings are attached to real life experiences that echo the silent voice of so many.

Be prepared to find the rich blessing that lies within the rows of each chapter new mercies day by day. I declare that this book is the springboard that propels your thinking, enriches your life and shifts your paradigm.

*Bishop Melvin Brown*

*Pastor, My Father's House*
*Ministries*

# Introduction

I believe, Dear Student, that it is no coincidence that you picked up this book. It was written just for you. There is something that is said here or a shared experience that will allow you to receive the healing and deliverance that you need to live a full and whole life. God ordained it this way. This book is a pit stop on the road to your destination; you can be fed, refreshed, refueled, and strengthened for the rest of your journey.

As you go through each chapter it's imperative that you are open and honest and really take time to work through each area that's covered and continually assess every area of your life. There may be things that you are uncomfortable with and don't want to think about or share with others but healing and deliverance starts with exposure.

I'm learning this even more as I write this book. I am a talker, I love talking but I am not a sharer; I do not share my life or experiences with others. I have a therapist for that. You won't find me in the grocery store talking to a stranger about anything personal. Although when I'm out and about many strangers talk to me about their personal lives. I can have a conversation with someone for hours and that person will leave not knowing any more about me than when the conversation began. I, on the other hand, will know their whole life story.

Maybe you're wondering why I'm telling you this. I first started writing this book in 2012. Bishop Melvin Brown of My Father's House Ministries in Charleston, South Carolina asked me to put something together for a women's mission. The church had started ministering in a low income apartment complex for women and children. I greatly admire and respect Bishop Brown and was excited that he'd asked me so I immediately started working on Shifting Paradigms. I was doing pretty good, had an outline and the first chapter completed when news came that one of my favorite uncles had died. I was very sad. After coming back from attending his funeral in Louisiana I didn't feel like writing anymore. When you write you're kind of in your own head and I needed a break from thinking. About 6 months later one of my great aunts died. I had great respect for my aunt and had actually followed in her footsteps by getting a master's degree in Education and planning to get my Ph.D. in Education also.

Experiencing so much loss really put me off my writing game I really didn't want to continue the book because I just didn't feel like writing anymore. But God had you in mind. He knew that at this point in your life you would need the words that He inspired me to write. He knew they would be relevant and life changing for you. So although it took me over a year to start writing again, it' all in God's perfect timing because the day that this book hits your hand is the day that your life will begin to change.

When I started to write again God spoke to me and said "it's time for the rest of the story". It brought to mind Paul Harvey back in the day on the radio when he would take you a little deeper into a news story and his tagline was "and now the rest of the story". I started having visions of speaking before crowds of women, which really didn't bother me but what bothered me is that I was telling them things that I would only tell my therapist. Every time I would envision myself speaking to the crowd I would be letting all of my secrets out of the bag. I was exposing myself. I talked to God about this because I felt I could be effective without having to share my life so openly with others. I have preached and taught for years but I haven't had to tell all of my business. From time to time the Holy Spirit would move me to share with someone and I would give them a piece of my testimony and that was okay but I was not okay with this tell all.

I really tried to convince God that it wasn't necessary for me to share personal things to be effective, I stopped having the visions so I felt maybe I'd made headway. Plus, I hadn't been invited to any speaking engagements anyway so I decided that I'd cross that bridge when I got to it. Needless to say that was not God's plan. He wanted me to tell the rest of the story here in this book. Every chapter that has anything about my personal life in it was written after I thought I had completed the book. During my review, I began to add more to some of the chapters and the more I wrote the more I opened my own life. God said to me, "How can you relate to them if they don't know your story?" How will they know that you've sat where they sit, in grave clothes, surrounded by ashes, wanting to lie down and give up, considering suicide, even contemplating homicide, feeling so down and so low that it took all of your strength just to lift up your head. He reminded me that I was trying to be strong, trying to be everything for everybody but neglecting myself. I looked like I had it all together but I was really empty, lonely and dissatisfied. I didn't know how I would make it but I decided to live for Him and I made it. He also said, "You are an overcomer, you broke through the pain, the depression and the disappointments and you live victoriously."

I remembered that God did not save, deliver or heal me just for me and what was the point of going through all of that hell if I wasn't going to use it to help someone else avoid it or come through it. I did not come to this easily and I wasn't as resigned as I may sound; I was still kicking and screaming. I didn't tell my entire life story but I'm glad that I did share some things because there is healing in sharing. There were still areas in my life where I needed full deliverance and as I began to write about and think about them I was able to basically "write out" the pain and hurt.

God is so amazing and awesome. He knows just what we need and how we need it. He knew that I needed more deliverance in areas that I never focus on and He knew that you needed to know that you are not alone and that there is light at the end of the tunnel. I pray that as you read this book and go through the lessons that you will begin to see your life change in a miraculous way, that you will be transformed by the renewing of your mind and allow your paradigm to shift.

To get the most out of this book I recommend that you do it in a group or at least with one other person. Hearing others' experiences can help you open up and share your own or realize that you're not alone. Being responsible to someone else also keeps you focused and on track.

If you are interested in going through the book with a group and having someone facilitate, an instructor guide is available. You will be amazed at how dynamic a group setting can be for growth and change.

Write me and let me know how this revelation and inspiration from God blesses you.

*Your Sister In Christ,*

*LuVara R. Prudhomme*

# CHAPTER 1

## *Shift My What?*

- ➤ What obstacles will challenge your commitment to going through this course? _____
  _____
  _____

- ➤ How can you overcome these obstacles? _____
  _____
  _____

- ➤ What are your priorities? _____
  _____
  _____

- ➤ How will you manage your priorities while going through the course?
  _____
  _____
  _____

- ➤ Complete Entrance Survey and give to instructor or e-mail to info@yourmindshift.com if you're completing the course solo.

  - ➤ Homework: Read **Chapter 2, What Does My Past Say About Me**

# Course Survey (Entrance)

Name:
_____

What do you expect to gain from this course?
_____
_____
_____
_____

Do you have a relationship with Christ, if so, how would you characterize it?
_____
_____
_____
_____

What areas do you think you're weak in (i.e. walk with Christ, family dynamics, relationships, financial stewardship etc.), why?
_____
_____
_____
_____

**What areas do you think you're strong in (i.e. walk with Christ, family dynamics, relationships, financial stewardship etc.), why?**

_____
_____
_____
_____

**What would you like to change most about your life?**

_____
_____
_____
_____

**What are your most pressing problems right now?**

_____
_____
_____
_____

**What help can others provide?**

_____
_____
_____

# CHAPTER 2

## *What Does My Past Say About Me*

### LESSON I

➤ **Repression and Suppression**

- Repression definition - Repression is the unconscious exclusion of painful impulses, desires, or fears from the conscious mind.

- Suppression definition - Suppression is the conscious exclusion of unacceptable desires, thoughts, or memories from the mind.

**What have you repressed?** _____

_____

_____

_____

**What have you suppressed?** _____

_____

_____

_____

➤ **Examine each coping mechanism below, in the table write down the coping mechanism you used, how you used it/what you did (behavior) and how you should have handled the situation or can handle the situation (solution). Be realistic and honest with yourself.**

## COPING MECHANISMS

- Acting out: not coping – giving in to the pressure to misbehave.

- Adaptation: The human ability to adapt.

- Aim inhibition: lowering sights to what seems more achievable.

- Altruism: Helping others to help self.

- Attack: trying to beat down that which is threatening you.

- Avoidance: mentally or physically avoiding something that causes distress.

- Compartmentalization: separating conflicting thoughts into separated compartments.

- Compensation: making up for a weakness in one area by gaining strength in another.

- Conversion: subconscious conversion of stress into physical symptoms.

- Crying: Tears of release and seeking comfort.

- Denial: refusing to acknowledge that an event has occurred.

- Displacement: shifting of intended action to a safer target.

- Dissociation: separating oneself from parts of your life.

- Emotionality: Outbursts and extreme emotion.

- Fantasy: escaping reality into a world of possibility.

- Help-rejecting complaining: Ask for help then reject it.

- Idealization: playing up the good points and ignoring limitations of things desired.

- Identification: copying others to take on their characteristics.

- Intellectualization: avoiding emotion by focusing on facts and logic.

- Introjection: Bringing things from the outer world into the inner world.

- Passive aggression: avoiding refusal by passive avoidance.

- Performing rituals: Patterns that delay.

- Post-traumatic growth: Using the energy of trauma for good.

- Projection: seeing your own unwanted feelings in other people.

- Provocation: Get others to act so you can retaliate.

- Rationalization: creating logical reasons for bad behavior.

- Reaction Formation: avoiding something by taking a polar opposite position.

- Regression: returning to a child state to avoid problems.

- Self-harming: physically damaging the body.

- Somatization: psychological problems turned into physical symptoms.

- Substitution: Replacing one thing with another.

- Symbolization: turning unwanted thoughts into metaphoric symbols.

- Trivializing: Making small what is really something big.

- Undoing: actions that psychologically 'undo' wrongdoings for the wrongdoer.

## Coping Mechanisms

| Coping Mechanism | Behavior | Solution |
|---|---|---|
| | | |
| | | |
| | | |
| | | |
| | | |
| | | |
| | | |
| | | |

| Coping Mechanism | Behavior | Solution |
|---|---|---|
|  |  |  |
|  |  |  |
|  |  |  |
|  |  |  |
|  |  |  |
|  |  |  |

# CHAPTER 2

## *What Does My Past Say About Me*

### LESSON II

➢ What hurt are you still holding and pretending not to have? _____

_____

_____

_____

➢ What unforgiveness are you harboring? _____

_____

_____

_____

➢ Does the past overshadow your present? How? _____

_____

_____

_____

➢ **Complete *Worksheet A, Examining Myself***

➢ **Homework:** Read **Chapter 3, What Does God Say About Me**

# WORKSHEET A
# EXAMINING MYSELF

**Name three words that you use to describe yourself and explain why you chose the word.**

A.
_____
_____
_____
_____

B.
_____
_____
_____
_____

C.
_____
_____
_____
_____

**Name 3 of the biggest mistakes you feel you have ever made and the age you were when you made the mistake.**

A.
_____
_____
_____

age:____

B.
_____
_____
_____

age:____

C.
_____
_____
_____

age:____

**Where did you live and who did you live with?**
_____
_____
_____

**How would you describe your home/environment at that time?**

_____

_____

_____

**For each mistake write down why you felt you made the mistake.**

**Mistake 1**

_____

_____

_____

**Mistake 2**

_____

_____

_____

**Mistake 3**

_____

_____

_____

**Do you blame yourself for the mistake? If you do why do you blame yourself?**

Mistake 1: yes or no. if yes, why?

_____

_____

_____

Mistake 2: yes or no. if yes, why?

_____

_____

_____

Mistake 3: yes or no. if yes, why?

_____

_____

_____

**How do you feel the mistake is still affecting you now?**

Mistake 1

_____

_____

_____

**Mistake 2**

_____
_____
_____


**Mistake 3**

_____
_____
_____


**Which coping mechanisms did you use or are still using?**

_____
_____
_____


**What better ways could you have responded or can respond now?**

_____
_____
_____


**What do you think you need to make your life better?**

_____
_____
_____

**Identify ways that you can meet these needs.**

_____
_____
_____

**Additional Comments:**

_____
_____
_____
_____
_____
_____
_____
_____
_____

| I GET IT! |
|---|
| RELIVING THE PAST WHEN IT HOLDS SO MUCH LOSS AND PAIN IS NOT EASY BUT IT IS NECESSARY FOR HEALING AND WHOLENESS. |

# CHAPTER 3

## *What Does God Say About Me?*

### LESSONS III & IV

➢ Do you feel that God is always with you? How do you know?

_____

_____

_____

➢ What do you feel that God says and thinks about you? How do you know God's thoughts towards you? _____

_____

_____

➢ How do you define pain? _____

_____

➢ How do you define suffering? _____

_____

➢ Complete **Worksheet B, Identifying My Pain**

➢ **Homework:** Read **Chapter 4, Exposure**

# WORKSHEET B

# IDENTIFYING MY PAIN

What is my pain?

_____

_____

_____

Why do I feel I have this pain?

_____

_____

_____

How do I react to the pain (i.e. cry, get angry, scream)

_____

_____

_____

What did I do or not do to contribute to my pain?

_____

_____

_____

What type of help do I need for my pain?

_____

_____

_____

What do I need to do to stop my pain?

_____

_____

_____

What's keeping me from stopping my pain?

_____

_____

_____

What changes will I have to make when my pain is gone?

_____

_____

_____

Who else is affected by my pain?

_____

_____

_____

If a Christian, what scripture addresses my pain?

_____

_____

_____


Additional Comments _____

_____

_____

_____

_____

_____

_____

| I GET IT! |
|---|
| IT'S ALMOST IMPOSSIBLE TO LIVE PAIN FREE WHEN YOU CAUSE YOUR OWN PAIN. IF LIFE HAS NOT GOTTEN BETTER THE PAIN IS NOT A PART OF YOUR PURPOSE BUT KEEPING YOU FROM IT |

# CHAPTER 4

## *Exposure*

### LESSONS V & VI

➢ **How do you define accountability?**

_____

_____

➢ **What or who are you accountable to?**

_____

_____

➢ **How do you define responsibility?**

_____

_____

➢ **What or who are you responsible to?**

_____

_____

➢ Do you hold or have you held a position(s) of accountability or responsibility? If so, do you meet the expectations of the position(s)? If so, how? If not, how or why not?

_____
_____
_____

➢ Were the expectations realistic? If so, how? If not, why not?

_____
_____
_____

➢ Write a letter asking someone you've hurt for forgiveness

➢ Complete *Worksheet C, Overcoming The Past*

➢ Complete *Worksheet D, Exposure*

➢ Complete *Worksheet E, Forgiveness*

➢ Homework: Read **Chapter 5, Who Am I**

| I GET IT! |
|---|
| EXPOSING HURT, ANGER AND EMBARRASSMENT DOESN'T FEEL GOOD BUT ONCE IT COMES TO LIGHT YOU WILL BE FREE AND ABLE TO WALK IN LIBERTY. FORGIVING SOMEONE THAT HURT OR ABUSED YOU IS NOT EASY BUT IT WILL RELEASE YOU AND EVENTUALLY THE PAIN WILL BE EXTINGUISHED. |

## WORKSHEET C

## OVERCOMING THE PAST

Things that I own from my past:

_____
_____
_____

People I need to forgive for hurting me:

_____
_____
_____
_____
_____

Write a letter of forgiveness to two of the people that hurt you

# WORKSHEET D

# EXPOSURE

Hello My name is _____ and I_____

_____
_____
_____
_____
_____
_____
_____
_____
_____
_____
_____
_____
_____
_____
_____
_____
_____
_____
_____
_____

## WORKSHEET E

## FORGIVING MYSELF

**I forgive myself for**

_____
_____
_____
_____
_____
_____
_____
_____
_____
_____
_____
_____
_____
_____
_____
_____
_____
_____
_____
_____

# CHAPTER 5

## *Who Am I?*

### LESSON VII

- How do you introduce yourself to others?
  _____
  _____

- How do you define identity? _____
  _____
  _____

- How were you identified when you were growing up (i.e. nickname, pet name, etc.)? _____
  _____

- Do they think the nickname fit? Why or Why not? Are you still called by this nickname? Does it fit? _____
  _____
  _____

- Define losing your identity? _____
  _____

➢ Have you ever lost your identity? If so, how? _____
_____
_____

➢ Have you encountered situations where you acted contrary to who you thought you were or claimed to be? If so, describe the situation and your response. _____
_____
_____
_____

➢ How did you reestablish your identity? _____
_____
_____

➢ Make a list of every area of fear that is in your family.

- For each area of fear that you have listed ask
    - Where it came from?
    - When did it enter into your family?
    - Through whom did it enter?

➢ Complete *Worksheet F, Who Am I*

# WORKSHEET F

# WHO AM I?

Words that describe me:

_____
_____
_____

Words that I want to describe me:

_____
_____
_____
_____
_____

What changes do I need to make to be described by my desired words:

_____
_____
_____
_____

# CHAPTER 5

## *Who Am I?*

### LESSON VIII

➢ **How do you feel the world identifies you?** _____
_____
_____

➢ **How do you think God identifies you?** _____
_____
_____

➢ **Here are ways that God is identified; put the attributes next to each (i.e. provider, etc.) and where in scripture the attributes can be found.**

- Jehovah Jireh – _____

- Jehovah Rapha – _____

- Jehovah Tsidkenu – _____

- Jehovah Rohi – _____

- El Shaddai – _____

- Jehovah Nissi – _____

- Jehovah Shalom – _____

➢ **Read Job 38-41**

➢ Complete *Worksheet G, The Identified Man & Man In The Mirror Worksheet*

➢ **Homework:** Read **Chapter 6, Learning to Value Myself**

| I GET IT! |
|---|
| LOOKING INTO A MIRROR AND NOT KNOWING WHO IS LOOKING BACK AT YOU IS ONE OF THE WORST FEELINGS YOU CAN HAVE. REMOVE THAT MASK, YOU AREN'T WHO PEOPLE SAY YOU ARE, YOU ARE WHO GOD SAYS YOU ARE…CHOSEN, ROYAL, FEARFULLY AND WONDERFULLY MADE…THAT'S YOU!<br>I SEE YOU WITH YOUR BEAUTIFUL SELF! |

# WORKSHEET G

# THE IDENTIFIED MAN

Who am I claiming to be?

_____
_____
_____

What do I claim that my life doesn't reflect?

_____
_____
_____

What am I lacking?

_____
_____
_____

How do I get what I lack?

_____
_____
_____
_____

What needs to be a part of my identity?

_____
_____
_____
_____
_____
_____

How can I add these attributes to my life?

_____
_____
_____
_____
_____
_____

What changes am I willing to make in my life/daily walk with Christ?

_____
_____
_____
_____
_____
_____

## MAN IN THE MIRROR

There are many men in the bible that God used to carry out his purpose and do miraculous things. David has been called a man after God's own heart, Elijah walked with God, Abraham was called God's friend…we can go on and on. Who are you? Who do you most identify with in the bible? What attributes do you have that stand out? In this exercise examine a minimum of 10 men in the bible and identify ways that you are similar to each man or have some of the same attributes. This may help you understand more about your purpose and also encourage you in your walk with Christ. You can select more than 10 men but not less.

| MAN IN THE BIBLE/ ATTRIBUTES | MY ATTRIBUTES |
|---|---|
|  |  |
|  |  |
|  |  |
|  |  |
|  |  |
|  |  |
|  |  |
|  |  |
|  |  |
|  |  |

# CHAPTER 6

## *Learning To Value Myself*

### LESSONS IX & X

➤ **Do you think that God values you as a man? If so, in what ways?**

_____
_____
_____

➤ **Do you value yourself? If so, in what ways? If not, why not?**

_____
_____
_____

➤ **Do you value being a man? If so, in what ways? If not, why not?**

_____
_____
_____

➤ **Name characteristics that are inherent to men and no other entity.**

_____
_____
_____

➤ **How do these characteristics set you apart?** _____

_____

_____

➤ **In what ways do you impact the body of Christ?** _____

_____

_____

➤ **What challenges do you have in serving God?** _____

_____

_____

➤ **How can you overcome those challenges?** _____

_____

_____

➤ **Make a plan to tackle your challenges; don't overwhelm yourself, tackle them one by one.**

➤ Complete **Worksheet H, Gifts! Gifts! Gifts!**

➤ **Homework**: Read **Chapter 7, Curses**

# WORKSHEET H

# GIFTS! GIFTS! GIFTS!

What gifts do I have?

_____
_____
_____

What gifts am I walking/operating in?

_____
_____
_____

I'm not sure of my gifts but I am very good at:

_____
_____
_____

How can I use these areas to support my church or community?

_____
_____
_____

If I had my choice I would like my gift to be. Why?

_____
_____
_____


Last month, I operated in my gift by

_____
_____
_____


Next month, I will operate in my gift by

_____
_____
_____


I am obeying the Great Commission by

_____
_____
_____


I will make a commitment to obey the Great Commission by

_____
_____
_____

# CHAPTER 7

## *Breaking Curses*

### LESSON XI

➤ What "equals" love to you and where did that idea or thought come from (i.e. gifts, money, affection, etc.)? _____
_____
_____

➤ When you think of curses, what comes to mind? _____
_____
_____

➤ Do you think there are curses in your family? If so, why? _____
_____
_____

➤ Do you think that you have the strength, wisdom and knowledge to break a curse in your family? Why or why not? _____
_____
_____

➤ Complete **Worksheet I, Curses & Other Things** and the **Curb Your Tongue Worksheet**

# WORKSHEET I

# CURSES & OTHER THINGS

What generational curses do you think are still operating in your family? Why?

_____
_____
_____
_____
_____
_____

What curses have you spoken into your own life?

_____
_____
_____

What curses have you spoken into your children's lives?

_____
_____
_____

What curses have you spoken into your wife's/significant others' life?

___

In what ways do you speak life?

___

In what ways do you speak death?

___

Identify ways that you can curb/control your tongue?

___

## CURB YOUR TONGUE

Many times we speak before we think…Everyone is probably guilty of this but we must remember that life and death is in the power of the tongue (Proverbs 18:21). It may not be your intention to speak death or even life but it happens. This exercise will help you examine the words that you say, the impact that they have and encourage you to find ways to speak or act positively into situations.

| I say: | To: | Which causes: | Instead I could: |
|---|---|---|---|
| Example: You're too lazy | My son | Him to think of himself as lazy and don't put forth any effort in anything | Find out why he doesn't want to do certain things and if maybe there's a problem he's experiencing. |
|  |  |  |  |
|  |  |  |  |
|  |  |  |  |

| I say: | To: | Which causes: | Instead I could: |
|---|---|---|---|
|  |  |  |  |
|  |  |  |  |
|  |  |  |  |
|  |  |  |  |

➢ **Do you feel like you've been blessed or received benefits from your relationship with God? If so, what benefits?**

_____

_____

_____

➢ **Do you believe God wants the best for you? If so, find scriptures that back up your belief.**

➢ Complete *Worksheet J, Benefits!*

➢ Homework: Read **Chapter 8, Determining Who I Want To Be**

| I GET IT! |
|---|
| MAYBE NO ONE EVER SPOKE INTO OR AFFIRMED YOU BUT THIS IS YOUR OPPORTUNITY TO CHANGE YOUR GENERATIONS' LANGUAGE. LET LIFE GIVING WORDS FLOW FROM YOUR LIPS. SPEAK POSITIVE, AFFIRMING WORDS THAT BUILD. NO MATTER WHAT IT LOOKS LIKE…ALL IS WELL!<br>SPEAK THOSE THINGS THAT BE NOT AS THOUGH THEY ARE |

# WORKSHEET J

# BENEFITS!

Do you know the benefits that you have in Christ? Here are just a few, please write the definition of what you think each benefit means.

Add to the list.

Blessed

_____

_____


Highly Favored

_____

_____


Fearfully & Wonderfully Made

_____

_____


Righteous

_____

_____


Adopted

_____

_____

Sound mind

_____

_____

Grace

_____

_____

Mercy

_____

_____

Abundant life

_____

_____

Peace

_____

_____

Joy

_____

_____

Wealth

_____

_____

Father
_____
_____

Savior
_____
_____

Holy Spirit
_____
_____

Covenant
_____
_____

Eternal life
_____
_____

More than a conqueror
_____
_____

# CHAPTER 8

## *Determining Who I Want To Be*

### LESSONS XII & XIII

➢ Think about all of the people that you know, select two that you think are living fulfilled lives. Why do you think their lives are fulfilling?

_____

_____

_____

➢ Ask the 2 people that you selected if they are fulfilled and why they feel that way. Compare their answers with yours and put the similarities and/or differences here.

_____

_____

_____

➢ Are you living a fulfilled life? Why or why not? _____

_____

_____

- How can your life be fulfilling or more fulfilling? _____

  _____

  _____

- Do you have a 5, 10, 15 or 20 year plan? If so, what are some of the major elements of your plans? _____

  _____

  _____

- How did you decide on the plans? How did they come to be?

  _____

  _____

  _____

- Do you think that you need to consult God about your plans? If so have you talked to Him about them? If not, why not? _____

  _____

  _____

  _____

  _____

- ➢ **In the book, I talk about 5 truths that we must take into consideration when looking towards the future, are these truth important to you? Are they a part of how you look at the future? Why or why not? If so, how do you implement these truths into your life? If not, what do you take into consideration?** _____

    _____

    _____

- ➢ Complete *Worksheet K – Scriptures for Daily Living*

- ➢ **Take a moment to reflect on your daily life:**

    - Do the people that you work with know that you have a relationship with Christ?
    - Are you open minded to everything and everyone's lifestyle so much that no one can tell what your true values are?

- ➢ Complete *Worksheet L – My Foundation & Worksheet M – Keeping It Real*

- ➢ Compare answers on *Worksheets L & M with Worksheets F & G*

- ➢ **Examine for similarities and differences. Make necessary changes or adjustments.**

- ➢ **Homework:** Read **Chapter 8, Determining Who I Want To Be**

| I GET IT! |
|---|
| LIFE CAN BE SO CHALLENGING THAT SOMETIMES IT FEELS LIKE YOU'LL NEVER GET A BREAK. NO MATTER WHAT…LIVE FULLY! EMBRACE EACH DAY LIKE IT'S THE BEST DAY THAT YOU EVER HAD AND IT WILL BE. |

# WORKSHEET K
# SCRIPTURES FOR DAILY LIVING

1 Peter; 2 Corinthians 6:11-18; Romans 12:10-21; Romans 13:8-14 all outline how to have a Christian life-style. Go through the scriptures and identify those that you need to apply to your life and ways you can apply them.

Scripture:

_____

_____

Application:

_____

_____

_____

Scripture:

_____

_____

Application:

_____

_____

_____

Scripture:

_____

_____

Application:

Scripture:

Application:

Scripture:

Application:

# WORKSHEET L

# MY FOUNDATION

My daily scripture:

_____
_____
_____

Help:

_____
_____
_____

Strength:

_____
_____
_____

Guidance:

_____
_____
_____

Relating to Others:

_____
_____
_____

Peace:

_____
_____
_____

Love:

_____
_____
_____

Encouragement:

_____
_____
_____

Character:

_____
_____
_____

My Daily Plan:

_____
_____
_____
_____

# WORKSHEET M

# KEEPING IT REAL

Who are you when you're not in church?

_____
_____
_____

How do others react to you?

_____
_____
_____

What do others think about you?

_____
_____
_____

How do you dress for work? Play? Church?

_____
_____
_____

What image do you want to portray to others?

_____
_____
_____

What three words would your co-workers use to describe you?

_____
_____
_____

What are your priorities?

_____
_____
_____

How do you talk to others?

_____
_____
_____

# CHAPTER 8

## *Determining Who I Want To Be*

### LESSON XIV

➢ What are your strengths? _____
_____
_____

➢ What is your purpose? _____
_____
_____

➢ If you changed your lifestyle or began to walk in your purpose, what challenges have you faced? _____
_____
_____

➢ How are you overcoming these challenges? _____
_____
_____

➢ **Homework:** Read **Chapter 9, Living Purposefully**

# CHAPTER 9

## *Living Purposefully*

### LESSON XV

➢ **Complete *Worksheet N, PRAISE***

- You don't have to use every area that's pointed out in the book; you may only need certain areas. Adapt the exercise to you.

- You can use whatever acronym you choose for PRAISE

- There are no right or wrong answers this exercise is for you to map out a plan that works for your life.

- Be open to change

➢ **Homework: Read Chapter 10, Sustaining The Shift**

| I GET IT! |
|---|
| YOU MAY NOT ALWAYS KNOW YOUR PURPOSE OR FEEL LIKE YOU'RE OPERATING IN YOUR PURPOSE BUT DON'T GIVE UP...KEEP PURPOSEFULLY PLANNING AND YOU WILL FULFILL ALL THAT YOU WERE CREATED FOR. |

# WORKSHEET N

# PRAISE

This is your PRAISE Plan you can use whatever alternative words you want for the acronyms.

Goal for Daily Living:

_____

_____

_____

| | |
|---|---|
| P_____ | |
| R_____ | |
| A_____ | |
| I_____ | |
| S_____ | |
| E_____ | |

Goal for Occupation:

_____

_____

_____

| | |
|---|---|
| P_____ | |
| R_____ | |
| A_____ | |
| I_____ | |
| S_____ | |
| E_____ | |

Goal for Finances:

_____

_____

_____

| P_____ | |
|---|---|
| R_____ | |
| A_____ | |
| I_____ | |
| S_____ | |
| E_____ | |

## Goal for Health:

_____

_____

_____

| | |
|---|---|
| P_____ | |
| R_____ | |
| A_____ | |
| I_____ | |
| S_____ | |
| E_____ | |

# Goal for Relationships:

_____

_____

_____

| P_____ | |
|---|---|
| R_____ | |
| A_____ | |
| I_____ | |
| S_____ | |
| E_____ | |

Goal for Service:

_____

_____

_____

| | |
|---|---|
| P_____ | |
| R_____ | |
| A_____ | |
| I_____ | |
| S_____ | |
| E_____ | |

Goal for Witnessing:

_____

_____

_____

| P_____ | |
|---|---|
| R_____ | |
| A_____ | |
| I_____ | |
| S_____ | |
| E_____ | |

Other Goal:

_____

_____

_____

| P_____ | |
|---|---|
| R_____ | |
| A_____ | |
| I_____ | |
| S_____ | |
| E_____ | |

# CHAPTER 10

## *Sustaining The Shift*

### LESSON XVI

➢ **Complete Worksheet O, Reflections**

➢ **Complete Course Exit Survey and give to instructor if you attended a class or e-mail it to** info@yourmindshift.com **if you went through program alone.**

**Celebrate!!!!**

# WORKSHEET O

# REFLECTIONS

Which lesson helped me the most, why?

_____
_____
_____
_____
_____

What did I learn that I didn't already know?

_____
_____
_____
_____
_____

What did I learn about myself?

_____
_____
_____
_____
_____

What other student impacted me the most, why?

_____
_____
_____

What will I take away from this course?

_____
_____
_____
_____
_____

What changes have I made since being in the course?

_____
_____
_____

What plans for change have I made?

_____
_____
_____

## Course Survey (Exit)

Name:
_____

On a scale of 1-10 (1 being not effective; 10 being extremely effective) how would you rate the course? _____

What do you think would make the course better?

_____
_____
_____
_____
_____
_____
_____

Do you think your relationship with Christ has changed throughout the course? If so, how? If not, why not?

_____
_____
_____
_____
_____
_____
_____

Were some of your weak areas focused on in the course? (i.e. walk with Christ, family dynamics, relationships, financial stewardship etc.), If so, did it help you?

_____
_____
_____
_____
_____

Were you able to gain more strength and insight in your strong areas (i.e. walk with Christ, family dynamics, relationships, financial stewardship etc.), If so, in what ways?

_____
_____
_____
_____
_____
_____

What do you think has changed in your life since going through the course?

_____
_____
_____

Were your most pressing problems addressed? If so, how? If not, why not?

_____
_____
_____

Did this group setting help you? If so, how? If not, why not?

Additional comments

Thank you for filling out the survey, this information will be used to improve our program and will be shared with course facilitators and group leaders.